The Royal Mix-up

Written by Lisa Thompson
Pictures by Andy and Inga Hamilton

Clinker Castle was expecting guests.

A King and Queen from a far-off land were coming to stay.

The trumpets sounded.

"This must be them," said the Queen.

“Welcome,” said the King to the guests. “Make yourselves at home. Our castle is your home while you are here.”

“Zoodip,” said the guests.

“Zoodip,” said the Queen and King.

The royal butler led the guests to the dining hall for lunch.

The guests sat under the table and painted themselves with food.

“That must be how they eat in their far-off land,” said the King.

“We should try it too, in case they invite us for a visit,” said the Queen.

The King, Queen and Knight took the guests riding in the forest.

The guests sat on their horses backwards, pointing to the sky.

“That must be how they ride in their far-off land,” said the Knight.

“Then we should try it too,” said the King. “We might be invited for a visit.”

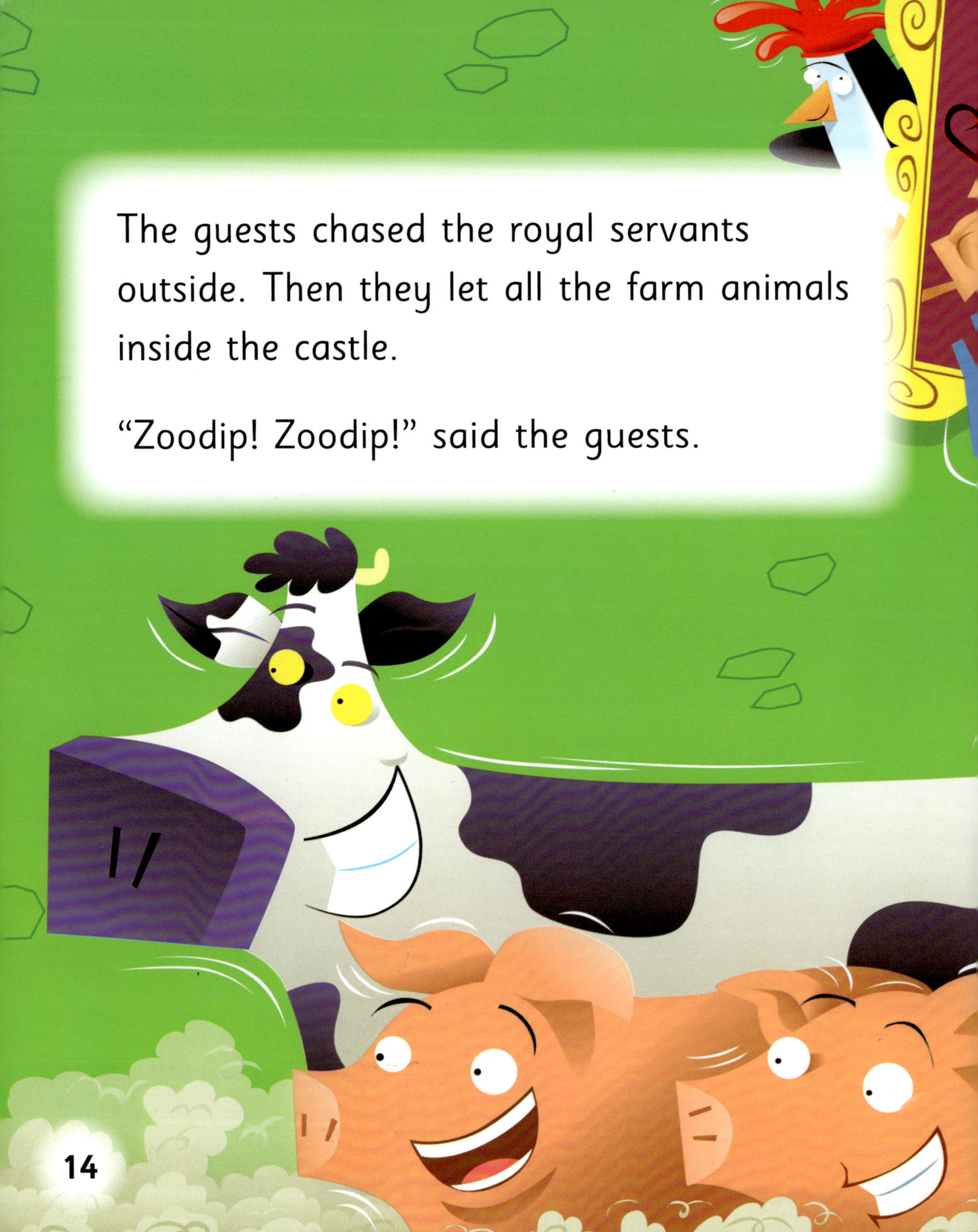

The guests chased the royal servants outside. Then they let all the farm animals inside the castle.

"Zoodip! Zoodip!" said the guests.

The Queen was not happy. She was sharing her throne with a chicken.

“Zoodip!” said the guests.

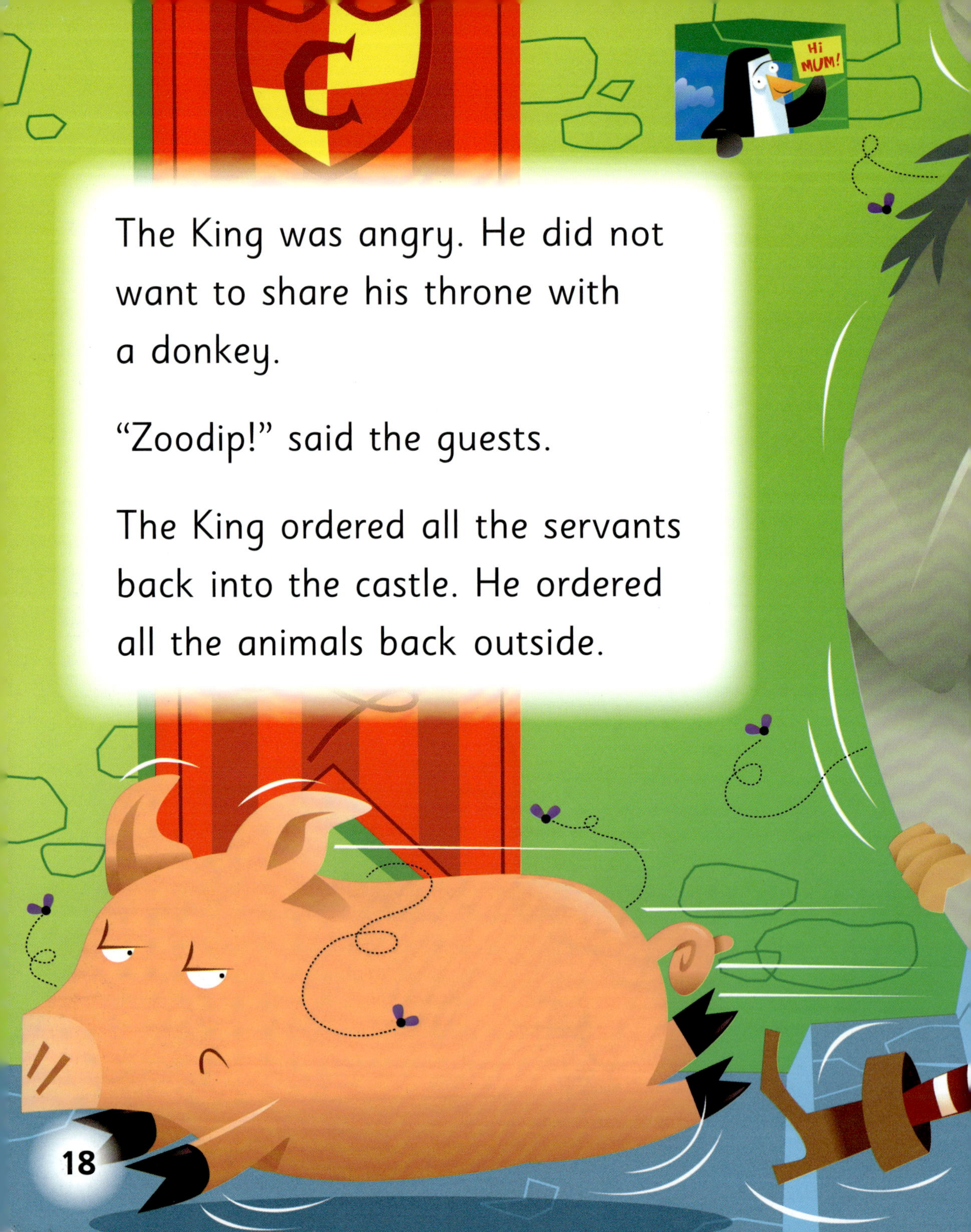

The King was angry. He did not want to share his throne with a donkey.

“Zoodip!” said the guests.

The King ordered all the servants back into the castle. He ordered all the animals back outside.

"Zoodip!" said the guests shaking their heads. They walked into the forest with the donkey and the chicken. That night, a strange light glowed above the forest.

The next day there was a knock at the castle door.

“Who are you?” asked the King.

“We are the King and Queen from the far-off land. Sorry we are a day late.”

“Zoodip?” asked the Queen.

“We do not understand,” said the guests.

“Thank goodness!” said the King. “Welcome! Make yourselves at home.”

Think About!
Why did the guests' habits seem strange to the King and Queen?
Why might your habits seem strange to someone who lives in another country?
How should you behave when you are a guest?